Poetry Tingles the Heart

Poems by Fiona Morris

Illustrations by Elizabeth Morris

Copyright © 2017 Golden Shells LLC
All rights reserved.

Published in the United States of America by
Golden Shells LLC, 550 Taylor Street, Ashland, Oregon 97520.

goldenshellsllc@gmail.com

Poetry tingles the heart. – First edition.

Library of Congress Control Number: 2017905745
Golden Shells LLC, Ashland, OR

ISBN 978-0-9983452-0-8

For My Brother

He is brave enough to handle anything.
His eyes show me a reason to see.
He has faith and wings and heart.
He gives me a reason to love and to care.

Contents

Introduction	1
Red Tree	3
Fairy Dance	4
Father's Day	4
The Boy Who Owned the Light	7
Boy at the Window	7
Tribal Dance	8
Fall Awakes	11
Asphodels	12
Native	13
Offspring	14
Open Your Hand to Love	15
Microphone	16
Poetry Is Not Rap	17

Poinsettia	18
That Kind of Dog	19
Beautiful Face	20
A Little Shy	21
Give That Girl a Turn	22
The Dawn Before	23
Sew the Seasons	24
Necklace	24
Painting with Flames	25
Lead Me to Life	26
Sixteen	26
The Gleaming	28
Like a Mountain	29
Love Is Good	30

Introduction

This book has been almost 10 years in the making. Fiona was just eight and half years old when she crafted her first poem. That first effort wasn't, in and of itself, a wondrous accomplishment—unless you look through the lens of disability. Fiona was born with Down syndrome and a serious heart defect. Her doctors didn't think she would survive beyond the age of two.

She proved them all wrong by getting through a difficult open-heart surgery at six months of age, and slowly but steadily growing stronger through her rocky first few years. She astonished everyone by reading at age three. It wasn't long after that she started sitting down to write about the wonders of life, and she hasn't stopped yet.

From the very start, my husband and I could see that she had a special way with words. We would look at one another in incredulity when she came up with lines like "reaching for metaphors in the soil." We wondered, was she channeling some unseen muse?

We could only surmise that it had been through osmosis or because we read to her so often, almost constantly since the day she came into the world. Like most children, she adored books and for many years would only eat while being read to. Once she began writing, her words revealed a sophisticated level of emotional intelligence and sense of wonder.

Nature has been the muse that's inspired much of her poetry, and she observes it with unexpected insight and a profound originality of expression that belie her young years. It is Fiona's writing, in turn, with its startling imagery, that has inspired much of my artwork. We first paired excerpts of her verse with my paintings for a series of greeting cards, and this book is a natural extension of that ongoing project.

We hope you enjoy reading the book as much as we did creating it.

Red Tree

Walking through the absence of life,
As a mysterious instrument plays
The melody of the Milky Way.

You feel a rush of cold air
As the river spirit prays to the red tree
With its roots reaching for metaphors in the soil.

Fairy Dance

All night we clap hands.
The children come to watch us.
They keep the fairy dance alive.

Father's Day

I am not perfect, but I will wrap my arms around your sorrows
Like the angel that sings you a lullaby.
All the stars shine for me when you smile.

I pray for you, a deserving prayer.
You've been in my dreams.
I will count on you forever.
The cocoon has not yet opened, but soon I will leave,
With heartwarming memories of father and daughter.

The Boy Who Owned the Light

Light against my dreary eye,
It felt like silt when first I met light to eye.
Now I, the boy who loves to be greedy,
want to own the light.

Boy at the Window

A rant of stars calls me.
I call back.
No one answers.
Peace in the silence.

Tribal Dance

As the fire has already been made and we are on our feet, we all dance 'round the fire.

We hold hands, and father plays the drum.

All the dresses twirling, and all the girls clapping.

All the boys singing the ancient tunes,

The inspiration from the gentle fox who hides his bushy tail behind a large tree.

We dance the dream of freedom, clinging like a leaf on a limb of a tree at the break of day.

There will be no more sorrow or fear.

There will be no tears once the day is come.

It's what the fox has given us.

Still a family, we pray more than we wish.

Fall Awakes

A gray velvet sky
Leaves change color—
Brown from red, orange, yellow, and green—
Falling like the stars you see within dream eyes.

Cool air smells crisp today
With the chirping of baby birds,
A light breeze swirls in
Through my window and
Lands on my arm like a butterfly.

Pies will come soon
Tasting of whipped cream and crust as
Pumpkin melts in my mouth
Like sweet candy on Halloween.

And I'll sip hot chocolate
When it first snows—
More white twirls of whipped cream!

A gray velvet sky,
Fall awakes with the open eyes of a white owl.

Asphodels

What's a poem without a title?
What's a bird with no wings?
Can they fly and not fall like the ball
that my two brothers play with?
My unwoven song of silence, like the asphodels
I have kept growing meekly in this jar.

Native

I am walking on the earth,
Gaia is all around me.
I see her nurturing eyes looking down on me.
I am her son.
Love is what she's given.
When I grow up, when I realize she's fled from my heart,
I pray sorrowfully for letting go of my Mother,
As though she will always remember me.

Offspring

This bird will never return to her nest.
Her chicks have learned to fly.
The rain comes from the falls, from the gray foam—
Told and taught be offspring.
I can picture her love in her cunning—
From the coldest, darkest pull,
From the tenderness in her heart.
This nest of eggs I hold in my hand, for a lifetime,
From the time a baby is born.

Open Your Hand to Love

Every year friends and family get older:
Cousins and brothers and sisters and mothers and fathers.

They stay with us forever.
Their dreams matter.
Their wishes matter.
Their futures matter.

We all sit around a table keeping light in each other's palms:
Giving, in both times of darkness and light.

Blow out your candles,
In the light and in the dark.
Open up your hand to love,
And a little more light comes out.

Microphone

Testing, testing for the first sound of success,
And receiving it back to you.

The first touch can make you shiver.
The first time you want to mouth the words that no one will understand.

Allow for the possibility of feedback.
You can move the switch up and down, but you can't force attention.

As you keep the sound the way it is, keep it a secret.
A microphone cannot form the words.

You're brave enough, but it can't force you to mouth the words for
the first time.

The standing ovation is you.

Poetry Is Not Rap

Pick up all the notes and throw them away, because poetry is not rap.
Turn off that beat, and give your mind a break.
It's not the rhymes you should mix up within a song and call it rap.

Poetry is a beautiful dove, gracefully perched on your arm.
And while you write, you get lessons in theoretical patience.
But rap carries nothing. It's a bird without wings.

Poetry tingles the heart of a sleeping velvet horse and makes the sun shine and Shimmer, until your ice cream starts to melt.

Poinsettia

Like another kind of exotic rose,
Bloomed in its beauty,
Unraveling like a blanket,
Covering fields of white snow.

That Kind of Dog

Jumping, wild beast . . .
Children run!
Palms sweating.
Out-of-range targets . . .
Danger resolved.
In that kind of dog, look away when it meets your eye.
Don't let it see you so terrified.

Beautiful Face

I'll give you a piece, but from my beautiful face, from my reddest lips.
How close can you get to me?
I cannot judge you, as precious as the petals in my small, pale hands.

A Little Shy

I am a little shy
To sit next to you and talk.
I am a little shy
To let your eyes gaze back at mine.
I am a little shy
To watch you paste a friendly smile.
I am a little shy
As your eyes sparkle, and mine sparkle back.
But I am too shy.
I can feel my fair skin turning red.
Please tell me, am I blushing?

Give That Girl a Turn

Give that girl a turn on the swing.
Give that girl a turn holding your pet rabbit.
Give that girl a turn telling the time.
Give that girl a turn on the trampoline.
Give that girl a turn to see your horses.
Give that girl a turn walking the dog.
Give that girl a turn holding the eggs.
And this time, she won't drop them!

The Dawn Before

When islands were far apart, stronger than I,
I wished to sail to a forlorn beach, ashore before dawn.
If I could spread my wings for flight,
You know I'd never come back.
I shall enter two forms of the meekest mind, to glide and fly and soar up ahead,
Far, far from yore.

Sew the Seasons

Take a spool, just one.
Pick a needle and thread, and start out slow.
Start with summer and go on with spring.
And third, sew winter and last sew fall.
Then pick up the scissors and cut off the thread
below your fingers,
And sew the seasons once more.

Necklace

My hands thread the beads.
My life, a piece of string
With wired and tired beads.
The colors are from an uneven land.
I put it on.
It's beautiful.

Painting with Flames

I am that star in the sky you want.
I'll give it to you if you proclaim that you wish to be brave.

I'll give you the full moon and Milky Way as it lights up your shining armor.
The clash of battle turns your flag blue.

Carrying the Milky Way, my flag is red.
With this bow are my sun darts.

My aim is like fire in a red circle.
I never miss.

I paint within the flames.
Every crackling step I make like tiny pieces of glass turned to smoke.

Now you carry a crescent moon.
I, a piece of a broken star that's half alive.

Lead Me to Life

For the scene to be set, show the visions inside this box.
The hopeless nights of boredom—forsaken.
All those days of weeping hearts—forsaken.

The spirits of the seasons ahead of us,
The passion inside our minds,
The beloved faith that changes our fates.

So, take this hand and lead me to life!

Sixteen

As sixteen baby birds learn to fly,
Sixteen butterflies flutter inside my stomach as a boy passes by.
A hint of certain unwelcome pain.

Sixteen teenage boys give me chocolate and flowers every motionless night.
How can I resist the magic of true love's kiss,
While me and my boy lie under sixteen stars?

The Gleaming

You know most days won't be like this.
Wake to a room of golden shells, gleaming, every day.

Like a Mountain

Your beautiful blue eyes staring back at mine.
I carry a bag full of hearing shells you have given to me.
They ring within and out my own ears.

I can see from your face that your light is not fading.
When you were young, I stood above you every day
like a watch dog.
Whenever you'd cry, I'd cry as well.

Now, you, like a mountain, you pick me up as my rocks
fall down into your ocean.
You are the King of my radiant smile.
I put on this face for you, and we both put on our
invisible crowns while leaning over

A glistening river of gold.

Love Is Good

Love is good.
It brings us hearts.
The glory of warm-hearted human hands.
Hold on!
Hold on to say love is good.

Fiona Morris is a poet and story-teller
who lives in Southern Oregon.
For more information, visit **www.fionawrites.com**

Elizabeth Morris is a self-taught painter
who enjoys creating images
that complement her daughter's poetry.